What's on the Ships?

Harley Chan

Ships come into the port.
Ships leave the port.
What's on the ships?

This ship is leaving.
Cars are on this ship.

The cars are for people in another country.
People there will buy the cars.

This ship is leaving.
Books are on this ship.

The books are for people in another country.
People there will buy the books.

This ship is leaving.
Computers are on this ship.

The computers are for people in another country.
People there will buy the computers.

This ship has come into port.
Shoes are on this ship.

The shoes are for people in this country.
People here will buy the shoes.

11

This ship has come into port.
Clothes are on this ship.

The clothes are for people in this country.
People here will buy the clothes.

This ship has come into port.
Toys are on this ship.

The toys are for people in this country.
People here will buy the toys.

Ships bring things into this country.
Ships take things out of this country.